# OPEN
## THE
# HEAVENS

*Isaiah 64:1 Oh that thou wouldest rend the heavens, that thou wouldest come down, that the mountains might flow down at thy presence.*

 By

## STEVEN A. KEYS

Written By: Steven Keys

Published By: Wisdom Writes Publishing Co. Houston, TX

Cover Design &Edited By: Wisdom Writes Publishing & Partners

ISBN 978-1-7337897-3-8

Facebook.com/Steven A. Keys (To give feedback and to connect with the author)

**Disclaimer:** The content in this book although rooted in biblical principles are the expressed interpretations and opinions of Steven Keys. Neither the publisher nor author shall be liable for any loss, damages, including but not limited to special, incidental consequential, or other damages.

**Permissions**

Please do take photos of your book for the purpose of review or to post on social media, but please do not photograph the entire parts of the journal. Please use the hashtag **#OpenTheHeavens** on all posts so that we can create a community of inspiration that is easily found.

# CONTENTS

# DEDICATION &
## ACKNOWLEDGMENTS

This book has been dedicated to my wife, Reella Garcia-Keys and my three children, Jezeniah, Mariah and Shamar. I thank each of you for understanding my calling and responsibility. I love each of you very much! I would be remiss not to acknowledge the two pillars that introduced and modeled Jesus before me, my late grandparents Deacon Charlie C. Keys and Claudia "The dreamer" Keys as well as my spiritual parents, Dr. Johnny L. & Gynetta Miller, and the late Prophetess Anita Radford for spiritually nurturing and developing me. I also want to thank God for my biological parents Mr. Steven Keys Sr., and Phyllis Smith. My mentors, Mr. Tommie Tate & Maria Sarno- Tate. I believe that this book is for every prayer warrior and intercessor who desires the heart of God, as well as for every believer whose desire is to see glory and revival break out in their city and nation. I would like to also thank Morgan Jefferson and Wisdom Writes Publishing Company for their excellent work, and last, but certainly not least I want to thank The Lord Jesus Christ for His grace and power.

# STILL WE STAND

We feel like we're in prison and no one can free us
But, then I talked with God and He told me the solution is Jesus
So, this is our reason our raison detre to keep breathing.

His life is our gateway so we must keep stepping
We believe in the Holy Writ that says no weapon formed against us shall prosper.
This is not a movie with no male actors and no stage production for an Oscar
This is a hurtful reality
Tears rolling down my eyes so much blatant murder and fatalities.

I know it feels like we can't breathe cause there's a knee on our neck
But in prayer I got a clear picture from God, He said "to right the wrong we must be just"
Just like Him with a question mark comes an answer
Where there's a lack of justice there's a picture from a camera.

We need a healer, His name is Jesus, He's a great shepherd with a perfect track record to lead us
Through the valley of the shadows of death, David penned it best you don't need 2020 vision
To see that this world is a mess, and yes we plan
I remember the words of Obama saying "yes we can" remove the color, so we can see
Stand united in the center of it all let love be the magnet that unites us.

Across the nation, there's one message we're all crying for equality and justice
So we must stand as one nation under God, not just on occasions
This shouldn't be complicated when all it is, is basic.

I am convinced that the world needs reformation we must ALL look to God
The Almighty One that made us now, can we breathe?????????????!!!!!!!!!!!!!!!!

*I dedicated this poem to my late best friend, **Raymond "T.S.D." Walson,** who transitioned on June 6, 2020. He was the first person that heard this poem and encouraged me to share it with the world. His life and legacy will continue, he left an indelible imprint in my life.*

# ENDORSEMENT

What sets Steven's Book apart from many other prayer and prophetic books is that it is laced with scripture and is used in its proper context. There is nothing more powerful than the written word of the Lord, it serves as the foundation as it should for the prophetic move of God. He calls the body of Christ into order in love and positions us to walk in the fullness of who we are in Christ Jesus. We are His masterpiece and His completed work!

**Robert H. Marshall Jr.**

Steven A. Keys, the author of this great book has been inspired to write after being touched by the Lord, to draw men closer to God, through prayer by the power of the ministry of the Holy Spirit. This book will change you from the inside out and expand your knowledge of prayer.

**Bishop Richard Oyengo**

**Power of faith in Jesus Christ ministries**

**The Glory Church International, Kenya.**

## CHAPTER 1

# THE SECRET PLACE

If you're always trying to be normal you will never
know how amazing, you can be.
**- Maya Angelou.**

*He that dwelleth in the secret place of the highest shall abide under the
shadow of the Almighty. - **Psalm 91:1***

It was on that rainy night of December 31, 2005, that changed
the trajectory of my life, and set me on course to pursue my
purpose and push my way toward accomplishing my God-ordained
destiny without a shimmer of uncertainty. It was a night that was
planned by my family and friends. We were doing what typical
families in most urban communities do in America on New Year's
Eve, and that's party until the breaking of the day. Doing it with
much vitality, enthusiasm, and hysteria. We had a galore of
outlandish ideas that were subjected to fail, because of the motives
behind our actions. My friends and I had made up our minds that
we were going to get so "lit'" that none of us would remember what
had transpired the night before, only to stumble into another year
lacking focus, vision, education, guidance, character and maturity.

We were on tiptoe anticipation about this big event, and nothing was going to prohibit us from what we deemed to be one of the greatest moments in our lives, because after all we were young and had forever to accomplish whatever we desired. At least that's what we thought. I remembered that night vividly it wasn't cold, it was a slight brisk in the air, the moon was full while beating upon the earth, there was a slight drizzle because of the rain. The stores were packed, and everyone seemed to have the same focus and goal in mind. That was to have an incredible time while being intoxicated to the point of not being able to remember what happened the night before. This was not a dream, but a mere reality that many of us had experienced year after year. So, the music began to play, the floor was filled in that small living room and we were bunched together like sardines in a can. Cigarettes were lit, the clouds of smoke had formed in the room, our voices were lifted as if we were auditioning at the Apollo in New York and everyone in a moment's time became their favorite celebrity without any timidity or chagrin. At the time it was bliss, it was a real moment for us trapped in a living room not knowing our purpose nor the plan of God for our individual lives. With only a desire to repeat the same cycle with a greater determination. There I was standing on the precipice of change while simultaneously being comfortable and content with who I was and where I was. Deep within me, I knew I had to change, and the good thing about it, I was willing to do it even if I had to risk it all. I realized that peace and tranquility aren't found in the place of comfort and familiarity as much as we may think. It's often times wrapped in uncomfortable decisions that enable us to discover our purpose in light of the challenges that may grow right before our very eyes. My grandmother had died earlier that year, May 8, 2005, on Mother's Day to be exact. It was the day prior to her transitioning that I stood by her bedside in that dim ICU room that she began to tell me sublimely that she was getting ready to leave this world. She said, "son my life's journey on earth will soon come to an end." she began to go into deeper details as she struggled to remove the oxygen mask from off of her face. With very little strength left in her physical body, she tried to lift herself up but to no avail. I was stunned and shook as I stood in utter disbelief as her words slowly left her shaking lips. I was mentally and emotionally unstable. I was wondering how was I going to process all of this and still function with normalcy on a daily basis. God will allow certain things to transpire in our lives so that we can see His providential hand work and perform the miraculous in our lives. As I tried over and over again to erase the dark scene from the memory bank of my mind, I found myself rehearsing it all over again.

My grandmother was a saved and spirit-filled woman who loved Jesus. She was persuasive in her witness for Him, a powerful truth teller, a template to model your life after, and an anointed gospel appraise dancer. I have no doubt that she's in heaven right now dancing on the streets paved with gold. As I helped her place the mask back over her face, so that her lungs could receive an adequate amount of oxygen, she closed her eyes to rest for a moment. That was a defining season of my life, now I realize that that moment was the seed planted within the soil of my heart that gave me the courage and resiliency to overcome that which appeared to be inevitable. Furthermore, it allowed me to embrace the days ahead, especially the day, December 31, 2005. Going back to that night in the living room where the music was playing my mind went back down the corridors of time, and there I found myself in deep conviction not knowing what was happening perhaps I had an inkling of an idea of what it could be. Then, I realized that my grandmother's death was the catalyst that would thrust me into a place that God had in mind for me before I was born.

I stopped dancing, I stopped drinking and I stopped mingling with my family and friends. As I gazed at my cracked Seiko watch the time read 11:30 P.M. we were just 30 minutes away from crossing over into the year 2006. I didn't quite understand what was happening to me, my mindset had been altered not by the alcohol (I had very little), and new thoughts began to emerge in my mind suddenly. I started hearing a calm voice tell me "you need to go to church". I was in agreement with the voice but couldn't quite understand this spiritual phenomenon that I was experiencing at that moment and time. I didn't realize that I was having a Jesus encounter. I knew I wanted Jesus, but I wasn't sure that He wanted me. My life at that moment was filled with sin, lying, cheating and everything else you probably could imagine. I felt ashamed and out of place. I left the living room and ran upstairs, and there I was alone in a dark small room (in the presence of God), emotional and nervous. While in that dark little room I began to cry profusely. After about 15 minutes I felt something come over me unbeknownst, Jesus revealed to me that He wanted me and that He wanted to use my life as an extension for His glory. I said to the Lord "If you get me out of 2005, I'll serve you for the rest of my life!" I realize now that humility gives birth to revelation. God can never be discovered; He can only reveal Himself to the one who seeks after him. I made a vow to Him that if He crosses me over into 2006 that I'd serve Him for the rest of my life. From that experience, little did I know that I was accepting my call into the ministry while divorcing a world I was so familiar with. That small little room became my secret place where I was born into the family of God.

We all need a secret place that will enable us to discover the reason for why we exist. There are uniquely arranged events that are licensed by God that He allows to invade the forecast of our lives so that we can reach the apex of our character driving us into the secret place where we can experience intimacy with Him. While being conformed into the image of His Dear Son, so that our lives can be changed as we thrive to advance His kingdom. The secret place produces strength, revelation, perseverance, intelligence, and other godly attributes. It's in the secret place where we can be naked before God about our struggles, shortcomings, failures and even our sins. So, that He by His grace can empower us so that we can march our way toward our purpose and destiny. After all, God sees all and He knows all. It's in our weaknesses and our conviction in knowing that He's omniscient that we can settle down, even while the odds are stacked high against us. Every person in the bible that was used by God experienced a secret place a defining moment of being shaped and carved for God's glory, a place where divinity met humanity and out that convergence was borne an authentic relationship with God that empowered them to change the course of ancient history. When the created meets the Creator change automatically occurs, the past of an individual is wiped clean, the stain of sin and death no longer has dominion over the individual, and freedom is initiated by God through the death, burial, resurrection, and ascension of His Dear Son. Moses' forty-year hiatus from Egypt was nothing more than a prelude that set him on course to experience God in a supernatural way. Preparing Him to walk into His prophetic assignment that liberated a nation that was oppressed and deprived of thriving socially, economically, and spiritually. Elijah's secret place became a cave and there he heard God in a still small voice that reactivated him in his prophetic assignment. Putting him on a distinct road to find his successor, so that his legacy would be solidified, while God's agenda would be perpetuated through Elisha. After Jesus was anointed with the Holy Spirit, He was driven into the wilderness by The Spirit to endure the temptation of the devil. The wilderness became Jesus' secret place of preparation before public ministry, His private devotion promoted Him to be publicly used by God to fulfill His redemptive plan for history. It's through that redemptive plan that humanity was provided a way of escape from the eternal judgment of God. Eternal life was granted to us through the establishment of the new covenant, which enabled us to have a relationship with God vertically while enjoying the beauty of fellowship with man horizontally (Acts 2:42).

The secret place is where God develops our character from within. There He takes us through a metamorphosis change. No one can see the internal supernatural workings of God, but nonetheless, the work is in operation. Until there is an internal change from within, we'll never be in a proper position to display the external change from without, which is connected to our salvation (Acts 2:38). Therefore, we need to incorporate patience and long suffering into the core of our being if we're going to experience the power of God anew in our lives. Prayer is not just a way by which we communicate with God, but it is an element that's needed in order to manifest what's in the invisible realm (heaven) into the earth realm. Many of us still struggle with developing a paradigm for prayer, because we haven't become common with the prayer paradigm that Jesus instituted (Matthew 6:9-13). So, we find ourselves in a state of frustration versus experiencing a blissful state of peace and tranquility. Prayer will never age, it has no expiration date. When God gave the earth to man to rule and have dominion over it. It was at that moment that God positioned man to have authority, influence, and power over everything that was physical. Which further proved that man was made in the likeness and image of his Creator. Giving him the ability to rule and exhibit authority. When Adam deliberately opposed the divine prohibition of God, by eating from the tree of knowledge of good and evil. The relationship between God and man was severed, thus causing a man to forfeit his relationship with God and from that point forward, man became spiritually dead no longer having the ability to communicate with God, because of sin. It was at that moment through a sacrificial institution established by God, Himself that an animal was to be slain by the shedding of blood, so that man's sin would be temporarily atoned for, which was only a shadow of what would be accomplished through Jesus Christ, The ultimate Lamb of God. The finished work of Jesus Christ has given us divine access into the presence of God (Hebrews 4:16) enabling us to come to Him with courage and tremendous faith. As a result of being the righteousness of God in Christ, we've been given access into a place that old covenant saints didn't have access to go into, because the price of redemption wasn't paid for at that time. Jesus, being our great high priest has established our spiritual position in God. We are seated in heavenly place, notice we aren't standing, but we're seated. We have a seat at the table with Christ we have a vantage point, we're actually looking down, we're over principalities and powers and this is our position forever. This gives us the legal spiritual rights to withdraw what we need from God in prayer. Our spiritual position is at the table with Christ (Ephesians 2:6) while our physical position is here on earth. We can penetrate dimensions through the channel of prayer in our secret place which produces within us the power, strength, and peace that passes all understanding.

Prayer gives the believer the ability to connect the earth with heaven. Prayer is our divine medium that crosses us over into the supernatural realm. We're not in it alone the Holy Spirit is our divine enabler helping us to accomplish heaven's agenda for us corporately and individually.

"Like the Spirit also helped our infirmities: for we know not what we should pray for as we ought: but the Spirit itself make the

intercession for us with groaning which cannot be uttered."
**Romans 8:26 (K.J.V)**

The Holy Spirit is the agent of prayer. Revealing to us the will of God, the character of God, the purposes of God, the grace of God and the love of God. It's imperative that we understand that we cannot pray without the Holy Spirit, He is the One who enables us to understand the depth of God's nature. When we've gained the adequate knowledge, wisdom, and understanding of prayer. It brings us into a realization of knowing that the constitution of our being (spirit, soul, and body) will be affected, thus producing supernatural results that could not be obtained otherwise. Prayer causes us to engage the presence of God intentionally, theologically, and reverentially. Knowing that through this divine channel it will provide sufficient revelation that will cause us to drive forward beyond our own ability by His abundant grace. Compromising for public fame with men can easily be an indication that one lacks a private relationship with God. Our private encounters with God will always produce public power before men. The time of our revealing is a direct derivative of us being concealed of God, He'll never promote what He hasn't sealed. When our lives become ethnocentric, that is having our lives totally centered around God, then we will understand the necessity of being connected to our secret place.

And in the morning, rising up a great while before day, he went out and separated into a solitary place, and there prayed. - **Mark 1:35**

Jesus understood the dynamic of prayer and the potency behind it and how it must take precedence over everything else. I believe the secret "sauce" behind Jesus flowing effortlessly in the miraculous apart from having the Holy Spirit without measure was His ability to remain in His secret place (prayer). He knew it was the medium by which He was able to establish the kingdom of God in the earth. Prayer is not only a partnership with God to accomplish heaven's agenda on the earth. Prayer also brings us into an agreement with God. The agreement is powerful on both ends of the spectrum be it good or bad whether it's pertaining to the kingdom of God or the kingdom of darkness. Satan's sole desire is to seduce us away from the allegiance of God so that we can't be as effective in efficient in our pursuit to advance the kingdom of God. Great godly men and women in the bible weren't considered great by accident. They understood that there was a great need to rend the veil between heaven and earth, which would ultimately produce the adequate revelation that would propel them deeper into the call of God for their individual lives. When Jesus Christ reigns preeminently in our lives, and when we're filled with the Holy Spirit. We're identified by heaven, which means that there aren't any restrictions on our access to the throne of grace. We don't have to do it alone, the Holy Spirit who is the agent of prayer helps us to navigate through the rugged terrain in our lives spiritually speaking. He is our helper, strengthener, advocate, and teacher (John 16:13). We must give Him access into our hearts and minds on a consistent basis in order to see the supernatural manifest in our midst. When we walk with Him the sick is healed, the dead is raised, the lame walk, the blind gain sight, and the gospel is declared with tremendous power. Often times through perils, problems, and oppositions we forget what God is able to do because our minds can be so consumed by what we're going through. That we find ourselves oblique headed in a totally different direction. Without the leadership of the Holy Spirit to stir us with His wisdom and knowledge. It is imperative that we understand that God's power is unlimited with Him being the Omnipotent One, He's sovereignty ruling over everything that He's created both visible and invisible. There's absolutely no lack in His ability to perform for us, He can do more for us than we can conjure up with words of what we can conceptualize in our minds. He's able to go beyond words, beyond our thoughts, what God is able to do is incomprehensible to the human mind. Like space and time God's ability to bless us extends infinitely beyond the rankings of men and extend beyond the world we can see with our physical eyes, and even the space and galaxies we can only imagine. The secret place isn't an ordinary place, but a place where things are born of the Spirit. Since you've entered in stay for a while until you're fully saturated and submerged in His presence and filled with His Spirit. Where are you?

## PRAYER

*Father, we thank You for the secret place that by our continual coming into it we're able to see your hands as well as behold the wonders of your glory. Give us solace in knowing that there's power, strength and peace in you, now reveal to us our purpose, so that you can be glorified in it as we walk by faith and not by sight. Take us to a place in you beyond what eyes have seen and ears have heard in Jesus' name, **Amen.***

## CHAPTER 2

# THE EXIT ROUTE

If you can't fly, then run.
If you can't run, then walk.
If you can't walk, then crawl,
But by all means, keep moving.
### - Dr. Martin Luther King, Jr.

*And Moses stretched out his hand over the sea; and the LORD caused the sea to go back by a strong east wind all that night and made the sea dry land, and waters were divided.. - **Exodus 14:21***

After we've entered our secret place and have become interwoven together with God while being conformed into the image of Jesus Christ. He strengthens us, rejuvenates us, empowers us, purges us, equips us, and enhances us for our life's assignment. I believe God, through the channel of prayer places in our spirits exit routes that give us the ability and advantage that will cross us over until our purpose and destiny are realized and honed. Think about this for a moment, whenever we're stationed in a certain place for a long period, and we find ourselves going through the same cycle over and over again. It's nothing more than a sign that we need an exit route. The more we're spending time in the presence of God we become more acquainted with His voice and become more sensitive to what He wants to accomplish in us and around us. Moses was a special kind of prophet not only, because he knew God face to face, but because Moses had in depth knowledge of who God is. Prayer enables us to have in depth knowledge of The One who created the heavens and the earth. Knowing His ways come from a deep yearning to know Him beyond the normative, beyond the regular scheduled program of life. It's beyond notoriety, beyond a platform, beyond public power, and beyond public preaching.

Exit routes are vitally important both in the natural and in the spiritual context of life. Moving beyond the familiar requires faith, it requires moving beyond the sphere of sensual perception and transitioning into a place of exercising faith that causes God to respond according to His Word as we are walking it by faith. Often times we find ourselves having to acquiesce through difficult seasons in life without having a complete understanding of what's transpiring. Sometimes only an inkling of an idea, but because God is Sovereign, we can stand on what He said with confidence and conviction. We would all agree that the Red Sea initially was not an exit route that would further take the nation of Israel toward their place of destiny, but in all actuality was a dead end seemingly designed by the enemy to prohibit them from progressing and moving into their purposed place. In the natural realm, there may appear to be dead ends in our lives. Dead end jobs, dead end businesses, dead end relationships, dead end careers, dead end visions, and even dead end marriages. I mean life can be really dark and bleak without any glimmer of hope or optimism that would settle us in a place of peace and tranquility while we currently stand in a place of uncertainty and doubt. But when we make a decision to pray by entering into the secret place that we discussed in chapter one we find out that God has a substratum plan for us both individually and corporately. That will enable us to press toward what He initially revealed to us in our secret place while communing with Him. Critical moments require us to prepare, plan and execute in a timely fashion all while being cognizant of the fact that we are not in it alone. Even in our darkest hour, God can still differentiate the dark from the light, because God works counterintuitive to our finite thinking.

He will allow the struggle to invade the forecast of our lives so that we can reach the apex of character. When we are entering a public building one of the things, we're exposed to the most are exit signs, and they are always lightened and marked with red lettering with the word EXIT. This conveys to us that we are not obligated to stay in one particular locality we have the liberty to move into another place as long as we follow the exit sign. I believe it is the same in prayer, there are exit signs that God reveals to us that gives us the assurance and holy boldness to make decisions beyond our own intellectual capacity. Because, we know our decision has been saturated in prayer, and as a byproduct of that we are able to step into new dimensions. That we could not have stepped into if the situation were otherwise. Exit signs produce revelation it reveals to us that what we see is not all there is to see. There is something on the other side, and we do not have to be trapped by our own imagination when we can move beyond what is. And move into what will be it is the same with Moses and his rod. It became a sign pointing an entire nation toward an exit route that crossed them over into something that they had not experienced before. Moses' rod was a "rod of revelation" unfolding to us a hidden mystery to those in whom he was responsible for leading and delivering. The moment he stretched out his rod it became the mechanism that pointed a nation into a divine direction. In deep and dark seasons in our lives, God wants to give us a divine direction that will dismantle anxiety, eradicate depression, and destroy even our insecurities. So, that we can cross over on dry ground it's not just about starting, anyone can do that, but it's about finishing strong despite our opposition. Finishing on the "right ground" can ultimately produce something that will have a generational blessing attached to it. As I contemplated on this rich theological narrative, I stepped aside from the expositional experience of it, and begin to use my "sanctified imagination". The enemy is approaching them with haste from behind, and the sea is in front of them and Moses begins to call on God. As Moses consulted God about the heart of the matter he stepped into his secret place, and God responded. Showing him that what he had in his hand would become the catalyst for immediate change for the realization of corporate destiny. There are certain things that God has placed within us, in our hands and in our minds that will provide security when the enemy is encroaching upon us. Could it be that the desperation has come because God wants to reveal to the world what He has placed within you. The only way He knows you can withdraw it out of your heavenly account. Is when desperation has been set in place, desperation could be our fuel that activates our faith revealing to us our spiritual power in the face of uncertainty and pain.

Contrary to popular opinion our pain is necessary, our frustrations are necessary, our setbacks are necessary and even our mistakes. It all brings us to a place where we must totally rely upon God, we were never meant to do life alone. As a matter of fact, doing life alone is the equivalent of having a car, but with no gas, in the tank, we end going nowhere. Accountability is born out a relationship that has been established by God. On another note, accountability helps us to embrace change and enables us to see from a different perspective. Embracing change is extremely important because we are continually experiencing change from a physiological, sociological, and psychological standpoint. Human scientist says that from the time we exit out of our mother's womb until the day of our demise we are affected by something called biological factors independent of the individual person. The mere fact that we cannot run as fast, jump as high and move as swift is all pointing to the fact that we are aging without being as cognitive of it as much as we should. No, I am not saying focus on death, because Jesus Christ's crucifixion, death, burial, and resurrection has taken care of that already. What I am saying is that we should focus on transition, transitioning requires a change of mind, heart, desire, focus, speed, stamina, skill, ability, direction, instruction and even intelligence. If, there is a transition, then be aware that there's change. The Holy Spirit is not just living in us, but He's come to provide us with present truth putting us in a position to demonstrate the character of Christ in a compromised culture. As we exit from one phase of our life into the next, God will give us the strength and endurance to fly against the contrary winds in our lives. God give us clear vision coupled with the ability that will position us to get to the place He has predestined for us to be on time. Destiny is in the eye of the beholder, but it will take faith to get to that particular destination. Yes, obstacles will come, burdens will get heavy, and detours will occur, but we must be convinced in our minds and settled in our spirits that better is the end of a thing than the beginning thereof. When God awaken our revelatory faculties He does it to change our self-perception, so that we're seeing like Him, and functioning like Him. The power of the prophetic word that has been uttered from eternity into time through God's chosen vessel is ultimately design, so that we exit from a place of incubation, and into a place of full maturity. Providing for us the clearance to be independent lacking nothing. In my time of walking with the Lord, I realized that growth is never easy, but necessary. When we come into maturity we, then by the grace of God step into our own unique anointing. God has tailor-fitted us with His anointing to get it done. We should never feel pressured to be like someone else or feel the burden to do it like someone else. All of us have a unique part to play in advancing the kingdom of God. Being empowered with the Spirit of God prevent us from procrastinating, procrastination is cancerous to our purpose, if procrastination is cancerous to our purpose, then unbelief and doubt is certainly our purpose placed in cardiac arrest. The exit route is a sign that God is not finished with us because there's another place He's trying to take us to as we submit to His will and believe Him for the promise. I often wonder at times myself why can't I have an easier route on the road to destiny? Then, I realize that the path that has been chosen for me wasn't predicated on how easy it would be, but more so on my willingness to adhere to God beyond my own comfort and convenience. Whatever God has shown you believe Him until He gives you an exit route, wait patiently in great expectation until what you see with your eyes can be touched with your hands.

## PRAYER

*Father, we look to you for strategies and exit routes that will ultimately lead to us fulfilling our kingdom purpose and destiny. We know it's not by might nor by power, but only by your Spirit that we're able to overcome the inevitable while we posture our hearts toward you. You are our hope and anchor we will be still and look with great anticipation of experiencing Your salvation in Jesus' name,* **Amen.**

## CHAPTER 3

# YOU CAN'T DO THIS ALONE

*Not by might, nor by power, but by my spirit, saith the LORD of hosts.*
*- Zechariah 4:6*

In the new testament Jesus taught Peter a profound kingdom truth in Luke chapter five that certain things that we need are placed in our environment. We just have to go further out and look deeper, in order to experience the supernatural that's within our reach. Could it be that God has given us a command to go deeper, but we are perplexed by what we see in our current experience in life. That we become crippled by the weight and pressure of having to keep going on when in all actuality we want to give up. This is why it's imperative that we understand that our faith in God alone is our springboard, our launching pad, our direct outlet that will connect us with the command of God. And out of that will spring our assignment for kingdom advancement. One of the primary things we will continue to learn in our walk with God is that when He's trying to teach us something new He'll allow us to come to the end of our own human knowledge. So, that we completely trust in

Him. Spiritual knowledge is acquired by The Word of God, prayer and through the revelation of God's Spirit. It is very possible to have a spiritual problem while trying to solve it with natural solutions. God will allow us to come to the end of what we know on this level so that we can enter the realm of faith on another level, and although we might not know it, we must believe God in it, we must believe God for it, and we must believe God through it. Abraham believed God and it was counted to him for righteousness (Genesis 15:6). When we have made prayer our priority there will always be a consistent flow of faith that will always lead to a perpetual flow of revelation that's being dispensed from God. When there's an inconsistent flow of faith, then there's an inconsistent move of God. When the hand of God is on our lives, it's a sign that the purpose of God has been known to us, and the power of God has been made available for us, the prosperity of God is given to us, and the personhood of God has been developed in us. We were never meant to go on our spiritual journey alone, the fact that the Holy Spirit is living within us is a sign that God is not only with us, but it is also pointing to the fact that we've been left on earth for such a time as this. To impact our generation and to penetrate the systems of the world with the gospel of Jesus Christ. This cannot be accomplished apart from us playing our part in prayer and articulating the mind of God (through consistent study of the Word of God). Our walk with God is beyond our physical senses, human reasoning, human science and even human psychology. This walk is spiritual the Hebrew writer gives us a persuasive promise and said: " And without faith is impossible to please him, for whoever would draw near to God must believe that

He exists and that He rewards those who seek Him." Whenever we make a decision to utilize the component of faith, God is pleased and we are rewarded. We could very well be on the verge of our biggest breakthrough, if we would just stay the course, if we'd just stay in His presence long enough to look like Him, long enough to behold his face, long enough to inquire of Him, long enough to sound like him, long enough to look like Him, long enough to forgive like Him, long enough to love like Him, and long enough to be transformed by Him. Transformation is born out of an assertive effort to long for Him even while we're broken in a sin-stricken state, even while we're in our embryonic stage of development God's plan and promises remain to be true irrespective of our current state of being. Whatever God calls us into it should make us nervous to the point where faith is produced and from there God takes us to a place beyond what we expected. See, we're never called to be alone and to try to do what God has called us to do in our strength the grace of God has been given to us so that we're adequately empowered to not only start but to finish strong. Jesus said, "my meat is to do the will of Him that sent Me and to finish His work."

Like David, our unseen victories are developing us for our public promotion. Character is developed privately while the fruit of it is seen publicly. It's in our faithfulness that God rewards us if we're faithful over a few things, then He'll make us ruler over many things. Crossing us over from a place of obscurity to a place of prominence, influence and power. In Zechariah chapter three Joshua and Zerubbabel have been transported from Babylon, and now God has them on new assignments that will enable them to experience His supernatural power and grace. They're now in Jerusalem responsible for re-building the temple, and in the midst of the project, they lose focus, sight, energy, and passion to finish the project. Because they were trying to do it alone without the grace and power of God. On many occasions we find ourselves trying to do it alone and it was never meant to be like that. God wants us to completely rely upon Him for everything, considering that He's our source. When we pray it's not only a sign of submission and humility before God, but it's also a sign that what needs must come from a superior source who has the ability to extend to us what we need, when we need it, and how we need it. Now, in order for that to materialize, we must be cognizant of the fact that we can't do it alone, and through prayer, we're positioned spiritually to receive of God the resources needed to move along in our daily lives. This is why Jesus said, "seek ye first the kingdom of God and His righteousness and all these will be added unto you." Many of us are trapped by our past, silenced in our present and blinded from seeing a promising future, and it is not until we silence our souls and really hear from God that we become all the more convinced that all of our life's experiences were meant to help us not hinder us. We must let go of our past if we plan on unwrapping our present and perambulate our way toward the future. When we make an assertive effort to trust God beyond what is in front of us, then His sovereignty is magnified creating a paradigm of faith that cannot be shaken. Trust is always revealed by our action and allegiance toward God rather than by our verbosity. The book of Zechariah teaches us both theologically and relationally that every one of us needs a Zechariah in our life to assure us that even in the toughest of times things can change in an instant. Proving to us that the timing of God far outweighs our ability to process all the events in our lives the way we desire.

When we are born again of the water and Spirit (John 3:5). There are many gifts that God freely gives us, that are revealed over a course of time. It is never God's intention or plans to call us into something without aiding and assisting us in the process. Now, what He has called us into will not reach its apex by us utilizing our own academia and intelligence. There must be a persuasion of The Spirit that we have enough to start and finish strong. Our help comes from above and not beneath this is why revelation is a key component because it provides for our clarity, and clarity is the byproduct of revelation. Whenever we're confused about something, we don't need peace as much as we need revelation, revelation removes the lid of limitation. If revelation removes limitation, then clarity is the plastic that suffocates confusion. The enemy brings confusion into lives, but with the revelation God gives us clarity. Allowing us to bask in His peace as He guards our hearts and minds through Jesus Christ. We'd all agree that God placed supernatural genius in Adam, but Adam was limited until God started asking Him questions. God wasn't asking Adam questions because He didn't know (He knows all things), but He was asking him questions to remove the lid of limitation by placing him in a position to speak by the Spirit of revelation. God told Abraham to look at the stars, if you can count them then that will be the number of your offspring, God was removing the limitation by giving him a revelation. Joseph's coat of many colors wasn't an ordinary coat, it was a coat of revelation. Light traveling at its highest velocity does not produce colors, but only produces light, now when light has been fragmented it produces colors. Joseph, having on a coat of many colors (revelation), begins to dream, and by way of revelation dreams a dream that shows him a vivid picture of his future. Prayer like Joseph's coat provides for us revelation that can foster us into a brand-new season infusing and empowering us beyond our own capacity. I believe the cure to disease is a revelation, the solution to our problem is revelation, the secret to marrying the right person is revelation, connecting with the right people come by revelation, and the solution for our sins came by revelation (Genesis 3:15). One of the primary reasons we need the Word of God because it reveals to us the mind of God. Zechariah who was a priest and prophet was perplexed by the vision that he received from the angel of the Lord (Zechariah 4:1-6) while being in the temple, but even in his ignorance, God granted him a revelation that would ultimately secure his understanding of what God was going to do with two men he had anointed and chosen for a prophetic work. We are not alone there's more with us than it is against us prayer will give us the eyes to see beyond the natural and see into the spiritual realm giving us confidence and assurance that we're safe and secure. The restorative power of God is always at work in the life of the one who is totally depended upon him (Matthew 5:6).

Restoration is a key component for reconstructing our lives. The anointing of God has the ability to restore us from our past so that we can reproduce and multiply in the present moment. Like Zerubbabel, many of us have become too weak to build what God has called us to build, because we aren't restored. I believe that as you're reading this book that you're marriage is being restored, your're children are being restored, you're finances are being restored, you're business is being restored, and most of all you're prayer life is being restored. God wants to restore the years that locust has eaten so that when we experience restoration, we will be more convinced that operating in God's will doesn't require for us to do it alone, but it does require for us to have the right community of believers to help assist us in our assignment. We don't have to do it alone, because there's plenty of grace to complete your assignment.

## PRAYER

*Father, we admit that often we try and drive down the road alone. By our own might, intelligence, ingenuity, and skill set. Today we ask for forgiveness and through Your forgiveness we realign ourselves with Your Word and Your will for our lives. We confess that we need You in our marriages, our finances, our businesses, as well as training our children in the fear of the Lord. we know that if You be for us then who can be against us? Grant us this petition in Jesus' name, **Amen.***

## CHAPTER 4

# THE QUANTUM LEAP

That's one small step for a man, one giant leap for mankind.
### - Neil Armstrong

*And he's leaping up stood, and walked, and entered with them into the temple, walking, and leaping and praising God. - Acts 3:8*

**M**oments of transition often times happen suddenly and swiftly with no preparation, no foreknowledge, and without full understanding of the present reality. Just an inkling of an idea that life as we once knew it has changed. God doesn't need permission from anyone in our families to anoint us for His designated purpose. He just needs our faith and radical obedience, so that our purpose can be grasped with our hearts and our destiny can be realized with our minds. Faith and obedience are the foundational pillars that enable one to journey in their walk with Christ with great expectation and hope. We can never come under the umbrella of obedience if we have not visited the household of faith. In other words, it is faith that pleases God (Hebrews 11:6), but obedience is what produces the blessing of the Lord (Due. 28:1-14). Faith is the starting point in our walk with God and obedience

33

is the conduit by which everything manifests from the spiritual realm and into the earthly realm. In lieu of what didn't work or what didn't go right, in spite of the vision board not taking on the accurate picture that was tailor-fitted in our minds. We must still acquiesce until change manifest in our lives.

We're not to remain where we are when God wants to dispense an adequate amount of revelatory knowledge for where He's taking us. Whether we're conscious of it or not we're on a journey, and when we establish ourselves in God's will we become one with Him, and what we couldn't see before He gives us the ability to see now. The scripture says "for we walk by faith and not by sight" walking by faith must supersede what our natural senses are conveying to us, as well as our ability to articulate that experience as well. When we're moving forward, when we're proliferating, when we're taking incremental steps forward in our pursuit to accomplish His assignment for our lives. We put ourselves in a position by showing the world in a demonstrative way what it looks like when a person has surrendered their entire being to God. We must understand that it's not the steps that we take that determines the outcome, but it's the One who's orchestrating our steps that determines the outcome. The scriptures say "The steps of a good man are ordered by Lord" as sons and daughters of God we're not to be driven by what we see. But, only be moved by what God has said, now from the time that God shows us our future until the time we arrive to it a lot will change. People will change and some will vanish as God makes room for others to come and occupy those vacant seats in the arena of our lives. We will change, our families

34

will change, our approach and perspective on life will change. This is why we can't allow despondency to become the catalyst that fuels the fire of anxiety and pain, but instead, we must allow it to help us realize that it's our moment. Sometimes our moment can be wrapped up in despondency and uncertainty, and if we don't have the wherewithal, the bandwidth, or faith to see beyond it, then we'll run the grave risk of making a temporary place a permanent place of dwelling. So, regardless of what it looks like right now. This could be the time where God is doing something completely different in your life, and when He desires to do something different. He'll send new people to confirm that it's Him that's in control. Men are just channels and conduits by which He flows through to accomplish His will, purpose and plan.

As it we're with the lame man that sat begging for alms at the gate of Beautiful (in Acts chapter 3). So, it is with some of us we feel stuck, impoverished, lame, stagnant, unproductive, purposeless, and unable to make any progress in our lives. It's important that we understand that Peter and John were on their way to prayer and because they were men of prayer God could show them things that He couldn't show ordinary religious people. Who only had a form of godliness while denying the power thereof this a picturesque view of prayer. Herein lies an incredible revelation that where we are lame in our lives, God has the power to instantly change our current situation forever by the power and the Name of His Son. God's sovereignty speaks, and it is uninfluenced by men thus showing us clearly the importance of time. It was the hour of prayer as Peter and John were making their way to the temple and this lame beggar became the focal point of receiving a miracle from God. Prayer to the believer is what oxygen is to the human body it enables us to function at optimum capacity. When we pray, we step outside of time and into eternity (to operate at optimum spiritual capacity), and we can hear, see, and speak on an entirely different level, because of the Holy Spirit who is living within us. So, as a result, we can take what God has shown us in eternity and bring it into time (by the aid and assistance of the Holy Spirit). Therefore as a believer of the Lord Jesus Christ we should be hearing on a different level, seeing on a different level, and speaking on a different level so that we're demonstrating the power of Jesus Christ wherever we may find ourselves. I am not ignorant of the fact that everything will happen in God's timing, this lame man was lame from his mother's womb. Having never walked a day in his life, but through the power of the name of Jesus Christ, he experienced a supernatural change instantaneously. Luke, the author of the book of Acts uses incredible phraseology to further reveal to us that this was in fact something beyond his ability to figure out. With him being a Greek physician (Colossians 4:14) he is very specific as to how this lame man went from a state of lameness to being empowered to take quantum leaps. Luke said, "and he took him by the right hand, and lifted him up: and immediately his feet and ankle bones received strength." Even as this lame man went from a state of lameness to a state of extreme mobility, I am persuaded that is what God wants to do with us! Through the power of the Name of Jesus Christ, we're able to take quantum leaps in prayer and in every other area in life, once we learn how to access the name of Jesus Christ.

Jesus said, "And whatsoever you ask in my name, that will I do, that the Father may be glorified in the Son." An answered prayer comes into fruition because God wants to be glorified through His Son, so that when we use Jesus' name in prayer it is not for personal pleasure, notoriety, and power, but the sole objective of us being able to utilize His Name is for the glorification of God and of His Son, Jesus Christ. If we are going to take quantum leaps forward, then there is a specific way that we must take in order to get the desired results. Just as the lame man received strength to do what he could not do before; I believe as we press on in prayer that God will empower us to do what we could not do in previous seasons of our lives. The evidence will be in the walking, leaping, and praising God. We are called sons and daughters of God (Romans 8:14) meaning that we bear the nature and characteristics of God. When we operate the Name of Jesus, being led by the Spirit of God we are functioning in a supernatural authority that is greater than any other authority that we may come face to face within the natural and spiritual. Taking quantum leaps are tied to prayer and the utilization of the Name of Jesus Christ. The president's name is great, a prime minister's name is great, Michael Jordan, LeBron James, Kobe Bryant, Denzel Washington, Barack Obama, Martin Luther King, Jr., and so many other names are great. But none of those names can compare with that of the Lord Jesus Christ, His Name, His reputation, His authority, and His power far supersede the normative. Could it be the reason why we have not taken that quantum leap is because we've been looking for others to do what only the Name of Jesus Christ can do when we approach God in prayer. Our lives can be so unpredictable and spiral out of control without any warning. While our lives can be out of control God is always in control. Dr. Paula price said "the more out of control God appears to be, the more in control He is" because God works counterintuitive to the human mind, He will allow things to become drastic only to reveal His glory and power. Transitioning from obscurity to prominence, from mediocrity to mega, from poverty to prosperity, and from rejection to acceptance is predicated on our ability to pray with confidence in God, competence of the scriptures and being led by the ministry of The Holy Spirit. God wants us to take quantum leaps forward are you ready? Are you willing? Are you completely convinced that, that is what He wants to do for you? If, so then get ready to take quantum leaps toward your destiny in Jesus' Name!

## PRAYER

*Father, in Jesus' undefeated name we thank and acknowledge that it's You who gives us the ability to take quantum leaps forward. Redeeming the time for us as we utilize the new opportunities for Your glory and the advancement of Your kingdom. We thank You for Your miraculous power and we know that You are the Lord, and You change not, and that Your power is working in us both to will and to work Your good pleasures.* **Amen.**

## CHAPTER 5

# PRAYER AND PROPHECY

If I find myself a desire which no experience in this world can satisfy, the most probable explanation is that I was meant for another world.

## - C.S. Lewis

*For the prophecy came not in old time by the will of man: but holy men of God spake as they were moved by the Holy Ghost.- 2 Peter 1:21 (K.J.V.)*

God's power is unlimited (Ephesians 3:20). He is the Omnipotent One who is sovereignty in control over everything that He has created both visible and invisible. There's absolutely no lack in His ability to perform on our behalf. He can do more for us than we can perceive with our eyes or what we can put into words, and we can do a lot of that. God's ability is oftentimes seen when we come to the end of what we know or what we can accomplish. The objective behind this is simplistic in nature it's so that God can get the glory there's direct parallelism as it relates to how the operative power of God flows and how His Word compliments it (Jeremiah 1:12). I know you've probably never heard of this before, but prayer in and of itself will not change our situation, but moreover, it's whom we're praying to that makes the ultimate difference (Matthew 6:9). With God being our source, the all sufficient One who answers our prayer according to His divine will. The Word of God gives prayer the license to be legal in order to function the way that it was intended to function. After Adam broke the divine prohibition of God was, then that man's relationship with God was severed, afterwards, God instituted prayer as a way of fellow shipping and rebuilding a relationship with Him, prayer should not be viewed as something minimal and mundane but should be seen as a stream by which our words have the liberty to flow after being recycled by the Holy Spirit to accomplish God's intended purpose for our individual lives. Prayer is beyond words the commencement of it is borne out of the Spirit of God. The same power that raised Jesus Christ from the dead is currently at work in our lives enabling us to operate in a capacity that normally we wouldn't be able to operate in. Being filled with The Holy Spirit is not just for speaking with new tongues, being filled with the Holy Spirit is not just for preaching, prophesying and or moving in the miraculous power of God. What we must understand is that being filled with the Holy Spirit is a down payment on our future inheritance. The fact that we're sealed until the day of redemption speaks volumes for the born again believer (Ephesians 4:30), it further proves that God has an incredible future for us that far outweigh anything that we've ever had to experience prior to our relationship with Him (let that sink in for a moment) Salah. Prayer is an information (revelatory) center that streams information from one realm (heaven) to another realm (earth) so that God's will, can be established making room for His kingdom agenda to be realized in real time. When we make a deliberate,

40

spiritually conscious- driven effort to the partnership with God through the channel of prayer. He, then reveal to us His plan and His agenda for our earthly affairs. Many of us haven't enjoyed prayer, because we lack the motivation and discipline that is required that will move us from the realm of normalcy and into the realm of the supernatural. Prayer requires a consistent desire to seek God beyond our past experience this is why there must be a constant seeking after God in order to maintain fellowship with Him. Revelation is born out of humility it takes a spirit of humility to trust anyone because we're relinquishing our will, ability and intellect into the hands of another person. With the intention of things becoming better and brighter than they were before (at least for most of us). True freedom is found in our willingness to come under the power of God even when it's beyond our comprehension and commonality. When we encounter the present power of God we will never be the same! Impossible right? The present power of God (that is His anointing) in operation in our lives can be our launching pad that helps us to gain ground that the enemy has stolen from us maybe because of ignorance, immaturity, sin, hurt, rejection or other mechanisms that the enemy uses to try to impede our progress. It takes faith to pray (Mark 11:22-24), once our faith has been activated we step out of time and into eternity as we enter the arena of prayer. On the contrary, unbelief will always be aggravated by the power of revelation. Where the miraculous has been demonstrated faith has been activated, and as a result, destinies are altered as the goodness of God is perpetually seen amongst His sons and daughters.

Harnessing a clear vision coupled with action can be utterly impossible to accomplish apart from solely depending upon God (Proverbs 29:18). When we authentically and practically trust God we're acknowledging His sovereignty as we personally submit to His Lordship. We gain adequate knowledge that will help us to penetrate every block channel of the enemy until we experience victory. The surpassing revelations and visions that the Apostle Paul had of The Lord Jesus Christ were beyond average and certainly, it positioned him to be a yardstick and template for generations to come. Although Paul was skilled with his hands in writing he was also wired by The Spirit to have an impeccable prayer life. He lived and breathed in the electrical, transformational, life-changing atmosphere of prayer! Prayer keeps us attuned to the spiritual realities and the persuasiveness of God's distinguished voice. When we don't know what to do and what decision to make, we must be still! God said "be still" this is not a suggestion; this is a command to be followed (Psalm 46:10). There are a variety of components that are borne out of stillness. Clarity is borne out of stillness, knowledge is borne out of stillness, and wisdom is borne out of stillness. Our next set of instructions from God may not come from another human being but could easily be given from a place of "stillness". If we can find the gumption to embrace this dynamic it can easily catapult us from where we are, and into the place where we should be. While all things are consistently moving, and while many other things continue to be unsettled, we must allow our place of "stillness" (that is our place of prayer) to evolve us, until we're conformed into God image and manifest His glory. Life is a process and out of that process, our purpose is gradually revealed to us as we take incremental steps forward. Reaching our destination will not be obtained easily neither will it be gained through passivity. Landmarks are good, but they only remind us that we're still in a familiar area in our lives. God will allow us to be vulnerable, shaken, and sometimes even unsettled in our spirit, because He knows in His infinite wisdom. That it's in our vulnerability that the modicum of our faith is demonstrated, and His character is revealed in us.

Theologians and Bible scholars believe that Jesus prayed for about three hours every morning, before starting His day (Mark 1:35). There was a ceaseless devotion that Jesus had with the Father that caused Him to function at the highest human capacity. Jesus was able to perform consistently in the miraculous not because He had the anointing without measure, not because He was virgin born, and not because He is the Son of God (all of that is true). But what allowed Jesus to perform with regularity in the miraculous was that He knew the importance of communing with the Father. I believe if we take on the approach that Jesus took, then we'd be further along the road that God has us traveling down. Certain things God has not delivered us out of because He has a strategic plan to take us through it. However, I am convinced that lasting movements are derived from effective paradigms placed in motion during the right season. The right paradigm can initiate a movement that can affect generations for centuries. Pentecost created a movement (the birthing of the Church Acts 2:1-4), and from that movement, a paradigm was established that has won millions of souls into the kingdom of God up until this point in history. Prayer and prophecy have a unique way of connecting with one another although they are two different agencies. When they are properly interwoven together it produces the will of God. A prophetic word is a word that is given in real time that is ultimately complemented by the written word. In other words, prophecy is God "finishing" what He started. This is why it's imperative that we become one with God because if we become one with God it places us in a position of becoming one with His Word. And God's Word will never return to Him empty, but it will always accomplish the purpose that it was intended to accomplish upon Him releasing it (Isaiah 55:10,11).

A prophetic word has the propensity to change the course of our lives and redirect us down a different road to destiny. A true prophetic word will not fall to the ground when it penetrates the earth realm (that is coming through another person), but it will be planted in the heart of the receiver in seed form. Once it has gone through the germination process and has reached its fulfillment, then what was once invisible. Becomes a reality in our realm of existence (understanding). When God releases a prophecy it's an indication that He has a purpose that He wants to accomplish, and prophecy is one of the conduits by which He reveals His purpose to a person, city and or nation. If you've read the bible for any length of time you will quickly come to the conclusion that God is a wise strategist, and that His Word is filled with endless revelation. Exposing His mind, the imperfection of humanity, and the life of His Suffering Servant (Jesus Christ). God will use everything to accomplish His kingdom purpose in us, this is why what you and I are carrying is not only intended to shake our sphere of influence but is also designed to help restore other people's lives that seemed to be bogged down by divorce, bad decision making, rape, molestation, poverty, anxiety and many other painstaking events in life. God can take us from a place of stagnation and comfort and give us a prophetic promise. Out of that same promise, He develops us for the promise by challenging our faith to go beyond what our natural eyes can see (1 Cor. 4:17-18). Whenever God gives us a prophetic command it is always tied to a vision that has not yet materialized in the earth. The journey that we must take to see the prophetic promise can only come into fruition when our spirit, soul and body have formed a legitimate covenant. That is when every entity of our being is on one accord. Although the journey can be challenging the reward always outweighs the hardships and challenges that come along the way. When a seed is planted it is a sign that its future is secured. Everything that God does, He does in seed form, but a seed must be planted in the right environment. A seed must go through the proper germination process and a seed must die so that its potential can satisfy its purpose. Jesus likened Himself to a seed he said "truly, truly, I say to you unless a grain of wheat falls into the earth and dies, it remains alone; but if it dies, it bears much fruit." (John 12:24) Prophecy is the seed planted while prayer is the water that sustains the seed that has been planted. This is why if we receive a prophetic word from God it must be nurtured (watered) with prayer. Prayer is what condition the heart so that the prophecy can be received and managed well by the recipient. Prayer, when utilized causes us to have the right response to what God has said about us. When we are pregnant with prophecy the place of prayer must be our safe haven and incubator that further develops us from one stage to the other while remaining in high expectation of what God has spoken to us. Although we are still in the waiting room of life.

The late Derek Prince said "The gift of prophecy is the supernaturally imparted ability to hear the voice of the Holy Spirit and speak God's mind or counsel. Prophecy ministers not only to the assembled group of believers, but also to individuals." prophecy establishes edification, exhortation, and comfort (1 Cor. 14:3) to the church (or believer), Christ's body on earth which is the microcosm of the kingdom of God. Often times God will use a prophet or another believer to release a prophetic word to an individual. That is one of the many ways God changes our self-perception. And through prayer, we are able to hone the prophetic word until we're changed by it. We need a prophecy to flow consistently in our lives because it is one of the means by which God can speak (in the present moment) so that our lives are impacted for His glory. The Holy Spirit is the One who gives us the ability to prophesy with confidence, competence and control (1 Cor. 2:9-10). As one of God's prophesies you're placed in a unique position to be God's mouthpiece in the earth conveying a kingdom message that has the propensity to change and redirect the course of a person or people group's destiny. God has not only filled us with His Spirit to think like Him, but He's also empowered us to speak His Word (Psalm 45:1) for Him. When a word pierces the earth's atmosphere and finds its place in the heart and mind of God's prophesier. It is done with one intention, and that is to change the destiny and purpose of an individual or group of people. A prophetic word from God provokes a response from the receptor. When a person receives a prophetic word it is God's intention that it provokes a change from within (the heart) then causing him or her to be in a position to access the benefits of God as they walk in radical obedience (Deut. 28:1-14). The role of God communicating through His chosen vessel is so that we walk (live) by faith and not by human logic and reasoning. The prophetic word is potent and carries with it the weight of God's glory, our faith continues to elevate as we continue to hear the prophetic word (as well as the written Word) and obey it. We are either walking by faith or we're walking by sensual perception (the flesh) when we walk by sensual perception and not by faith. We find ourselves trying to conceptualize the things of the Spirit with our human logic versus trying to gain understanding by faith. This is why prayer and prophecy are like "Siamese twins" you can't have one without the other. As we continue our spiritual journey let's embrace our prophecies as well our prayer life. God's plan is much greater than our plan and often times its through the means of prophecy that He's able to reveal that plan from eternity into time.

## PRAYER

*Father release the prophetic grace upon the Body of Christ afresh and a new, so that destinies are altered to your will, and purposes are realized. Give us hearts and minds that is wired with heavenly wisdom and revelation, so that we accurately convey your message to all people groups in the earth. So, that valleys are exalted, and mountains and hill tops are made low and the crooked paths are made straight, and rough places made plain. Your mouth has spoken it. We want to see our generation change, and we believe through your grace upon us that it will position us for a great prophetic move of God in the earth in Jesus' name. **Amen.***

## CHAPTER 6

# GOING INTO GETHSEMANE

A Sacrifice initiates a move of God.
**- Choco De Jesus**

*Then Jesus came with them to a place called Gethsemane, and said "sit here while I go over there and pray.".- Matthew 26:36*

**P**rayer is the lifeline for all believers worldwide. Prayer is our breathing apparatus that provides us with the spiritual jumpstart that we need so that we're more Spirit-driven as we set our eyes upon Jesus who is the author and finisher of our faith. The place that our Savior resorted to the most was a place called Gethsemane, Gethsemane literally means oil press. The meaning carries a great deal of spiritual significance, considering that the name (title) Christ means Anointed One. With Jesus being divinely anointed, appointed and commissioned by God. That places Him in a unique position to not only be the prophet, priest, and king (fulfilling each office succinctly) of His people but moreover, it qualifies Him to be our present day High-priest who is alive forever making intercession for us (Romans 8:34). That is a good reason why we should not worry as a matter of fact worrying is a sin, because it exposes our distrust in God and in His supernatural ability to perform on our behalf. It has been said "when life throws you lemons make lemonade" as a consequence of having been born again and being filled with the Spirit of God it should help us to face the challenges of life with great optimism knowing that God will always bring His Word to pass in our lives. Gethsemane was a place of solitude and comfort for the Savior, and of course, it brought Him great hope during His darkest hour. Right before Jesus was about to fulfill the redemptive plan of God, He went to a place called Gethsemane. He was in deep distress, agony, and so much emotional pain that he couldn't escape it even through prayer, because it was God's will that He would suffer, be crucified, buried and be resurrected on the third day morning. In Luke's gospel account he said "and being in an agony he prayed more earnestly, and his sweat became like great drops of blood falling down to the ground." Jesus was experiencing what a human scientist called hemosideros is also called bloody sweat this normally happens when the human body is under extreme stress and anxiety. When the human body reaches a certain level of mental stress and anxiety the capillary blood vessels that regularly feed the sweat glands are torn, and as a result, the sweat glands push blood out causing it to be mixed with sweat (bloody sweat). When Jesus found Himself in His darkest hour, He didn't call down a legion of angels as a matter of fact He prayed the same prayer three times. The only thing He received in that great moment of anxiety and stress was an angel coming to strengthen Him so that He could fulfill the prophecies that was written about Him. I can remember that horrific morning June 6, 2014, while getting my daughter

49

dressed for school. I got a call from my mother and she said "Steven, your brother was in a car accident" I told her that I'd call her back because I was getting my daughter dressed for school, so I hung up the phone. With much shock and charging, she called back, and said "NO!!!!! This is serious!! He was on his motorcycle this is really serious!!!". So, I drove over to her house to pick her and my sister up to go to the hospital to see how he was doing. As I pulled up in front of the house, they came toward the car with their faces full of tears. My mother said, "your brother is died!" I couldn't do anything, but ride to the hospital in silence all while being numb to the fact of what had just transpired. At that moment I felt like I was having a Gethsemane experience it seemed surreal, like a dream. So much pain, hurt, bewilderment, pressure, emptiness, frustration, etc., but while in prayer I could physically, mentally, emotionally and spiritually feel God strengthen me. Although the experience of what happened to my brother will forever be etched in my mind, the grace of God will forever be realized as well.

If you have not had a Gethsemane moment eventually you will. It is a place where God affords us the grace to overcome the impossible while He gives us the courage to drive through the rugged terrain of life. God doesn't care about how we feel as much as how we think the Bible is filled; with examples that reveal the mind of God. We have access to the mind of God, which is the Word of God. I believe once we have the mind of God on the heart of the matter, He gives us the adequate amount of grace (empowerment) to make decisions and adjustment that are needed so that we can prevail in His purpose for our lives. After all, it is solely about the purpose and glory of God. God can get glory out of a catastrophic event. The crucifixion, death and burial of Jesus Christ was for the glory of God, Him dying on the cross pleased God, the Father. From that event in history, our eternal destiny would be sealed. Certain things God will not change, because it is all part of His divine plan being revealed so that we (the church) could be a part of something that we could not be a part of otherwise. I can remember growing as a child and I would be playing basketball in the backyard with my cousins and the next door neighbors. And right when the basketball game would be getting really good, my grandfather, Deacon Charles Keys would yell "Steven get in the house and bring your cousins!" the screen door would slam hard because of the springs. When we would enter the house, he would have us to sit and anoint us with oil. We did not know why we were being anointed with oil all we knew was that it was strange. My grandfather would explain what the oil represented and then proceed to pray for us by laying his hand upon our heads. He would say to us "you all don't understand it now, but in the future, you will" through prayer he was planting seeds (the Word of God) in us that would soon manifest into a harvest. I believe God used him to pave the way for me in ministry. When I accepted my call into the ministry, he was the first person to know. He was like my spiritual navigator while many of the kids I grew up with went to jail or became victims of gun violence and drugs. I knew it was through my grandfather's intercession that God preserved me for such a time as this, and yes, I am grateful for it. Although my grandfather went home to be with the Lord back in October 2014, I believe there was an importation of the prayer mantle giving to me from him. Prophet Kris Valuation of the Bethel Church in Reddington, California once said "The anointing is for the man, but the mantle is for the mission". We continue to pray because God has each of us on a spiritual mission, and while we are on this mission, we need a mantle, the power of God to be present. The prophet Elijah in the Old Testament wore a mantle which was a loose fitting garment that was symbolic of the power and strength of God upon his life.

I believe that as God prepares us, He is going to give us the mantle of prayer as He builds us up in the garden of Gethsemane. We cannot run from Gethsemane if we are going to gain victory at the cross. Redemption does not precede isolation and consecration although they complement one another there is a divine order that God has set in place for His own purpose. You will notice that Jesus did not skip the garden of Gethsemane to go to Calvary, there was much needed time for Him to spend with the Father before going to the cross. There's much that God wants to show us in our "garden of Gethsemane" that can connect us with the right relationship bringing about a sudden transition as God anoint our heads with oil and our cup runs over. Continents, countries, nations, cities, and communities can all undergo a transformation if we stand in our place of intercession and not be moved by the currents of the water and winds of life. How can two walks together unless they have agreed to meet? When we make a faith filled decision to agree with God. Governments will change and leadership across the board will be affected. As we pray in the spirit, I believe secrets will be revealed by God (according to psalm 25:14). If we want the

Heavens to Open in order that we might experience the change that we desire, then there must be a sacrifice that goes beyond our convenience, understanding and comfort. God is after our faith because that is the only thing that can please Him (Hebrews 11:6). Let us arise and shake the heavens, so that the mountains may quake at the presence of God.

## PRAYER

*Father, as we embrace our Gethsemane help us to understand that suffering is of necessity if we're going to reign triumphantly. We thank You for stretching us beyond our place of comfort, so that we are dependent upon You for breakthrough and deliverance in Jesus' name,* **Amen.**

## CHAPTER 7

# THY KINGDOM COME

When one door closes, another opens; but we often look so long
and so regretfully upon the closed door that we do
not see the one which has opened for us.
**- Alexander Graham Bell**

*Thy kingdom come. They will be done in earth, as it is in heaven*
*- Matthew 6:10*

As the Apostle Matthew puts his pen to parchment and begins to write by divine inspiration of The Holy Spirit. He does so with the kingdom of God being at the forefront of his mind, and Jesus being the King of that kingdom. He starts His book out by giving us the historicity of The King, Jesus Christ in fact he takes us down 42 generations (see Matthew 1:1-17) in order that we may be convinced that this Messiah-King is legit and can be traced through a genealogy. Matthew understood the audience in which he was writing to, therefore his central focus was to express the kingdom of God through Jesus Christ. The Greek word for kingdom is basileia it is tied to royal power, kingship, dominion, rule and or authority. When we experience the spiritual transformative work of the Holy Spirit (John 3:1-6) in our lives we were not just qualified for heaven, but we were literally transferred into the kingdom of light to be agents of that kingdom, as a result of the finished work of Jesus Christ. Being part of the Kingdom of God means that we are to be initiators and not procrastinators, initiators can see what needs to be done in the earth and with the assistance of the Holy Spirit, they're able to execute the will of God until the earth becomes a replica of heaven. Procrastinators on the contrary may have the foresight and spiritual intelligence, but they don't possess the wherewithal to work their assignment until it's complete, instead of taking advantage of time procrastinators become abusers of time. And eventually, they fail to accomplish God's intended purpose for their individual lives.

Apostles, prophets, evangelists, pastors, and teachers (Ephesians 4:11), as well as prayer warriors and intercessors, are initiators of the Kingdom of God. They desire to see heaven on earth and continually they put God in remembrance of His Word (Isaiah 43:26). When we pray "Thy Kingdom Come" we are desiring God's reign, rule and royalty to be established in a particular geographical location. Wherever we may find ourselves it is our duty as a citizen of the kingdom of God to initiate His kingdom purpose. Isn't that what Jesus did? Jesus rarely talked about the church (it was a mystery to the Old Testament prophets), but He placed a tremendous focus on the Kingdom of God (Matthew 4:17). Even after His resurrection and being with His disciples for forty days (Acts 1:2,3), He continued to speak to them about things pertaining to the Kingdom of God. When we do our due diligence and study the scripture, we realize that God gave Adam power and authority, He literally gave Adam a kingdom (planet earth) to govern and rule, but by default and him breaking God's divine prohibition, Satan took full advantage of his vulnerability through the lust of the flesh, lust of the eyes and pride of life. The kingdom that God gave to Adam was usurped by Satan himself so in Jesus' first advent (the second Adam), He came with the sole intention of deliberately initiating the kingdom of God in a new and profound way. This is what Matthew is conveying to us as He witnessed Jesus firsthand on the Mount of Olives as He set down and taught (Matthew 5:1,2), which was His rabbinical custom. When we make a decision to pray, we're coming into perfect agreement with God in spite of how bad the situation may appear to be. Intercessors are God's gap fillers (Ezekiel 22:30) who have been empowered by God to see in the spirit, speak by The Spirit, hear by the Spirit, and move by the Spirit. Prayer is not optional, just like breathing isn't optional going a long period without breathing can result in loss of brain activity and eventually death. It is the exact same way when it comes to prayer going long periods without fellowship with God can prevent from us being effective, and if we fail to change that dynamic, then we'll eventually experience a disconnect in our pursuit of establishing His Kingdom in the earth.

Prayer has become an essential ingredient in my life. It has gotten me through some of the toughest moments in my life, I can remember some time ago when I was employed by H & M railway things, we're going well for me financially. Then, all of a sudden through a contract change. Which did not benefit most of us who were employed there. Things suddenly spiraled out of control really quick! So, quick that I did not have time to prepare for what had happened. Needless to say, I went from a steady shift to being on-call and eventually due to the lack of work, I had to file for unemployment. I did not know what to do, but I knew that it was a test of my faith, it was at that particular moment that I realized that the modicum of my faith was seen through the trial that I was currently facing. My oldest daughter at the time was just three years old and my wife was pregnant with our second child, and she was placed on bed rest by the doctor. Things appeared to be really bleak and dark for a young man who was trying to lead and feed his family. I can remember me literally crying before God (my tears became my prayer language) without clarity or insight on the heart of the matter. Prayer has been a lifeline for me, and through that trying moment, and me making a decision to trust God to provide and restore my family, I got a chance to experience Jehovah-Jireh. After coming out a prayer very emotional a couple of days went by, and I received a phone call from one of my colleagues whom I had not talked within months, because of the sudden lay-off. So, I picked up the phone and with much shock and amazement, I was told to call to New Jersey because the job had a big check for those who were laid off suddenly. At first, I wasn't going to call, but I asked myself a question "Steven what do you have to lose?" , after getting off of the phone I called New Jersey and after being on hold for quite some time a lady picked up the phone and we dialogued for a brief moment. She looked me up in the computer system and my name popped up, she explained to me that the funds were just sitting there waiting to be claimed. It is amazing how God will work things out at the right time for our good and His glory. After talking with her, I received a 4,000.00 check in the mail! I am not telling you this so that you can treat God like an ATM machine, but what I am saying is that prayer will initiate His kingdom to manifest on your behalf in more ways than one. Praying is not time wasted its actually time invested this is what Jesus was conveying to those followers of His day. It bears repeating even now to those of us in the 21st century. I am of the firm belief that the reason why Jesus was able to be as effective and efficient in His call to ministry was because He valued prayer. And had a profound revelation on how to incorporate the Kingdom of God in the earth. He didn't allow nothing or no one to prohibit Him from connecting with the Father this is why Jesus is our template on how to commune with God. The Olivet discourse (Matthew 5, 6, and 7) are all teachings on the Kingdom of God, but it is not until Matthew 6:9-13 that He gives us a prescription on how to connect with God, The Father through the mechanism of prayer.

Prayer will change our self-perception and enable us to come to the realization that we are of a chosen generation, a royal priesthood, a holy nation, a peculiar people the ones He has called out of darkness into His marvelous light. Do you know who you are? Can you see where you're going? Do you know who you are connected to? If, so why aren't you as confident as you should be? Why aren't you as strong as should be? Why aren't you taking those quantum leaps forward? Why are you allowing your past to disconnect you from your future? Why have you allowed excuses to hold you back? Why have you allowed that divorce to dismantle your ability to move forward? Why have you allowed rejection to be the dominating voice in your life? I know I have asked you a galore of questions, and if you cannot seem to answer them right now it could be because you haven't valued the secret place, the place of prayer. Where we experience the perpetual presence of God. All of us are in different seasons and stages of our lives and we are constantly changing and evolving every day. The Kingdom of God is within us (Luke 17:21) and through that born again experience we're able to see the favor and hand of God empower us to do what we can't do in our human strength. When a caterpillar becomes conscious of the fact that the season of its life is about to undergo a supernatural change it doesn't make a public announcement. It further embraces a private process; it undergoes what human scientist call a metamorphosis.

A metamorphosis change occurs when enzymes (called caspases) enables the body to be restructured leaving it with just breathing tubes allowing it to have just enough to survive in its darkest moment as it undergoes goes a change from within. As the caterpillar is in a private season it is isolated from the general population of its kind. In order that it may become that beautiful and fascinating butterfly. It must abide alone without any assistance, without companionship, without a confidant and without anyone to intercede on its behalf. The only way we can verify that the transformation was successful is when it musters up enough strength from within to break out of what it is currently encapsulated in (the cocoon). This is relevant to our spiritual

59

experience, because like the caterpillar if we are going to experience change it must start from within. God's Kingdom is spiritual in nature (Romans 14:17) and it must be experienced from within if we are going to manifest its power. A change from within occurs when there is a convergence, a convergence is when two separate entities (persons, individuals) merge together to accomplish the same purpose. When we received Jesus as Lord, we not only entered into His kingdom, but there's a supernatural convergence that positions us to accomplish a purpose that is almost identical to that of Jesus Christ (Matthew 28:18-20). True biblical and spiritual convergence is always accompanied by revelation. God cannot be discovered; He only reveals Himself to the one who's seeking after Him (Hebrews 11:6).

In the book of Hebrews (Hebrews 1:2,3) it reveals to us that Jesus is the authentic radiant expression of the personhood of God. That is to say that Jesus looks just like His Daddy (ABBA FATHER), Jesus is the complete revelation of God wrapped up in human flesh. When Jesus Christ donned human flesh, He was displaying to us a side of God's personhood that was mysterious to the prophets of old and even the angels. On many occasions when Jesus would heal someone, deliver someone from demonic oppression, and or raise them from the dead. It was at that moment that He was displaying an aspect of God's nature and power that Had never been displayed before in human history. Through those experiences which were witnessed by the general public and religious groups alike, many found themselves worshipping and following Him, due to the fact that He was walking in a level of revelation and light that was not known to man. When the Kingdom of God is demonstrated in our lives, we become light-bearers (Matthew 5:16) that replicate the authentic, miraculous, and life-changing power of Jesus Christ and His anointing. In the Old Testament when God revealed Himself to Moses (see Exodus chapter 3), it was with the intent of reestablish a kingdom, a theocracy by which God would be king and His people would come under the governing guideline of His constitution (Exodus 20:1-21). This was actually established by God through the partnership of Moses, the great delivering prophet of the nation of Israel. When God came into a covenant agreement with the nation of Israel a theocracy was inaugurated by God so that He could make visible that which was invisible to the human eye. In short, He wanted to display His glory and power through a people group who was willing to come under His governmental authority and leadership. Jewish historian, Josephus said, "the Jews were under the direct government of God Himself." The nation was only subject to God and no one else. This is vitally important, because if we are going to superimpose the power of God in the world systems, then we must come under His direct authority and power, by carrying out His principles and being led by His Spirit. The kingdom of God is within you, and often times God will allow certain things to transpire so that He can use them to demonstrate His kingdom's power and authority. He's already provided everything you need (2 Peter 1:3) to become all He has designed and created you to be. There are certain things that ONLY YOU CAN DO, you have been giving the grace and gifts so that His kingdom can come and His will, can be done on earth as it is in heaven. His kingdom is within you, and through prayer, you can make it visible in the earth.

## PRAYER

*Father, thank You for translating us out of the darkness and placing us into the Kingdom of your dear Son and through Him, we have redemption, the forgiveness of sins. Your kingdom come and your will be done on earth as it is heaven in Jesus' name, **Amen.***

## CHAPTER 8

# OPEN THE HEAVENS

Deeply embedded in the nature of man is the
spirit of rulership and authority.
**- Dr. Myles Munroe**

*Oh! That you would rend the heavens and come down, that the mountains might quake at your presence .- Isaiah 64:1*

The profundity behind the oration of the prophet Isaiah's cry (prayers) can be echoed by many of us today. With racism, sickness, disease (COVID-19), an imbalanced government, and an economic crisis at an all-time high. We are all crying for revival like Isaiah. We are asking God to intervene and intercede right NOW (open the heavens)! F.B. Myers said, "God cannot refrain His mercy if we cannot refrain our tears!" often times we need to take a self-inventory check of ourselves and see what we need to remove and what we need to add into our lives so that God can come in great glory and power. All God wants is a remnant of people who is willing to sacrifice time in prayer in order for Him to invade our space and eradicate the enemy's plan. When God revealed Himself to Moses on Mount Sinai (Exodus 19:17-18) it was extraordinary.

Mount Sinai was covered in smoke as the Lord descended on it in the fire, the people watched in fear and trembling at the awesomeness of the presence of God. As we pray and patiently wait on God, He will act on our behalf and show Himself to be our refuge and strength and very present help in the times of trouble. If we're going to experience God's power in our circumstances, then we must repent from anything that has prevented our close fellowship with Him. We cannot experience God's power without walking in purity. The prophet Isaiah understood this quite well as he gave us a clear message on who we are even on our best day. He said "we have all become like one who is unclean, and all our righteous deeds are like a polluted garment. We all fade like a leaf, and our iniquities, like the wind, takes us away."

Before God can open the heavens and perform miraculous deeds. There must be a confession of our sins (repentance) that results in a transformation of the mind that ultimately results in a transformation of action that brings glory to God. I am convinced that God wants to reveal Himself to the unsaved, and re-reveal Himself to the church. Often times miracles are done so that we can draw closer to God so that our relationship can be established from within that it can be visibly seen from a fruitful life without. We cannot experience open heaven in our lives without considering what we need to fix. When the Church is divided, schools closing, unemployment increasing, police brutality, wars, and people hating one another, primarily because of skin color. It's a sure sign that we need the heavens to open. God's plan is perfected in our weakness it's through understanding that dynamic that places us in an uncanny position to fulfill His awesome purpose in our lives. Jesus afforded us access into the presence of God when He became our kinsman redeemer and suffering servant through public humiliation (crucifixion & capital punishment).

"Jesus, when he had cried again with a loud voice, yielded up the ghost.

And, behold, the veil of the temple was rent in twain from top to the bottom; and the earth did quake, and the rocks rent." when Jesus fulfilled the redemptive plan of God, He provided for us a new way into the presence of God (Hebrews 4:16). It was the supernatural power of God at work to break down an old system so that the new could emerge through the redemptive and eternal work of His Son. Jesus' sacrificial work on the cross not only afforded us a seat in heavenly places (Ephesians 2:6) but also gave us direct access into the Holy of Holies. God's presence in us and on us is what makes us uniquely different from the world. If we are willing to pray, then God is willing to respond (Isaiah 59:1). He is not sleeping, He is not tired, not too busy attending to the needs of heaven, and not overlooking us. When we pray, we are stepping out of time and into eternity with the sole desire to see God's will execute in the earth realm. When we fail to pray, we have made a conscious (or unconscious) decision to take on life's circumstance with limited strength and vitality. The objective behind the heavens being opened is not so that we can experience His goodness only, but more to see God's splendor be revealed in the midst of chaos and confusion (Genesis 1:1-5). Where chaos and confusion are perpetuated it is an indication that there is an absence of the presence of God due to prayerlessness. Prayer is the medium by which God ordained for His own purpose and glory this is why we cannot afford not to pray. When we do not pray, we reject the medium through which God has established that affords us access to Him, so this is why it is critical that we pray, and pray His will (Matthew 6:9-13). Because apart from praying to Him, we disqualify ourselves from receiving what He desires to dispense upon us for His glory. A praying Church, a praying people, a praying person, a praying husband, and or praying wife can be more effective than a million people functioning in their highest capacity. The reason why they are more effective is that they have made a bold decision to invite God into their situation (Romans 8:31-32). And when we hold fast to the profession of our faith, it is by that same faith that God rewards us. We cannot be drunk with the wine of this age, but we must be filled with the Holy Ghost. Dr. Martin Luther King, Jr. once said "Use me God show me how to take who I am who I want to be, and what I can do, and use it for a purpose greater than myself." We must understand that a true anointing is not void of persecution. It is through persecution that God opens the heavens and produce what we could not produce, He is the Great producer and provider. Being pregnant with purpose can only be valued in the belly of someone who knows God and can wait on his timing to see what is on the inside manifest on the outside. When God has spiritually impregnated us with His purpose it is vitally important that we have the right response. I believe there is something hidden in you that God wants to reveal to the world, and it will depend on your response. Responding to what He said is a sure sign that prayer has become a dwelling place for you and not just a place that you visit every once in a while, when there is nothing else to do. God will open the heavens when we open our mouths and remind Him of what He said. If God has placed His Word above His own name, then when we use His Word, He has no choice but to respond to what He said. Experiencing God's presence is always tied to us declaring His Word. When the law of prioritization has been set in place (Matthew 6:33). We put ourselves in a position to perpetually bring glory to God, prayer isn't about persuading men, it's about "persuading" God if, there's a way to persuade God, I'd say it's simply by believing in His word and responding accordingly. We all will experience private frustration as well as public frustration, but if we wait long enough God will give us the mental fortitude, physical strength, and adequate answer that we need that will silence the whys so that we are properly position in the environment of clarity. If we are going to experience open heaven, then we must be convinced that we're part of a different government system, the Kingdom of God. It is the system that God has instituted, which carries with its principles, an agenda, supernatural power, and a King the Lord Jesus Christ. If you are part of this government nothing can stop you, nothing can harm you, nothing can overtake you, nothing can dismantle you, nothing can punish you, nothing can move you out of the way, and nothing can prevent God from executing His plan on your behalf. This is why the scriptures command us to watch and pray, prayer has to do with our heart's posture the heart is the engine that enables us to execute our will or the will of God (choose wisely). This is why it is vitally important that we guard our hearts, and not allow them to become contaminated by the world. No, we are not perfect, but by God's grace (through His, Son Jesus Christ) we are empowered to live a life that's peculiar and uncommon to the world. Knowing that we are fearfully and wonderfully made does not exempt us from asking God to search our hearts. It should be our desire as a result of being children of light to live in the light so that we are traveling down the right road. That leads us to accomplish our godly purpose and destiny. The heavens are open because the Holy Spirit has initiated the process, and as we grow in it, we will see change not only in our lives but in the lives of everyone that God will allow us to encounter. It is my prayer that you experience an open heaven as you live in God's perpetual light.

## PRAYER

*Father, we thank You for giving us the ability to approach you in prayer. We thank You for opening the heavens and providing for us in every area of our lives, we believe because you have opened the heavens that revival will break out and your glory will be revealed not only in us but all around us. We are asking that you release your glory, power, and wisdom until we are perfected into The Perfect man, The man, Christ Jesus,* **Amen.**

# ABOUT AUTHOR

Profound, prolific, prophetic, and fruitful are some of the adjectives that describe the ministry of God's servant, Steven A. Keys. He accepted his call into the ministry on April 6, 2006, and was licensed and ordained on August 11, 2007, under the leadership of Rev. Dr. Johnny L. Miller. He was born and raised in Chicago, IL, on the city's westside. With a strong desire to maximize his spiritual potential, so that he could be thoroughly equipped to advance the kingdom of God. He decided to further his education, in the fall of 2008, he received his certificate from Moody bible institute in expository preaching and teaching. He didn't stop there; he went on to Liberty Theological Seminary and received an A.A. degree in religious studies with an area of concentration in comparative religion. Afterward, he went on to receive his Bachelor of Ministry degree from Covenant Theological Seminary in Greenville, North Carolina in 2017.

He has his eyes set on obtaining a doctorate in theology. He has traveled both nationally and internationally, ministering the gospel of Jesus Christ. His heart and passion for justice and equity among all people, has positioned him as a bridge-builder between various cultures and generations. For over a decade, Steven A. Keys has faithfully been the proud husband to Reella Garcia-Keys and a devoted father to Jezeniah, Mariah, and Shamar.

Made in the USA
Middletown, DE
17 April 2021